How to Train Your Labradoodle

A Step-by-Step Expert Guide to Grooming, Caring, and Raising a Designer Dog from Puppy to Adult to Behave Positively

Finnley Crestwood

Disclaimer

The information in this book is intended for general guidance on training French Bulldogs. It is not a substitute for professional advice. Always consult with a veterinarian or certified dog trainer for tailored recommendations. The author and publisher disclaim any liability for actions taken based on the content of this book.

Finnley Crestwood

How to Train your
Labradoodle

Contents

Introduction

Did you know the smart and energetic Labradoodle was originally bred to be a guide dog for the vision impaired? It's true! These dogs were purposefully developed by Australian breeders in the late 1980s to combine the friendliness of the Labrador Retriever with the hypoallergenic coat of a Poodle. The goal was to provide those with disabilities a specially tailored service dog that didn't shed. The result was the highly trainable and intuitive Labradoodle that makes an amazing companion today.

I discovered this fact when researching breeds prior to welcoming my first Labradoodle into our family. I had fond memories growing up with our rambunctious Golden Retriever. Now with two young kids, my wife and I wanted an intelligent breed that would be gentle with the children yet energetic enough to match their activity levels. The Labradoodle seemed the perfect fit.

We brought home our caramel-colored Labradoodle puppy Max at 8 weeks old. He was the fluffiest pup in his litter who immediately bonded with our delighted children. As I gazed down at his sweet face, I made a commitment to bring out the best in this eager pup through compassionate, dedicated training.

Having trained retrievers previously for field work, I felt prepared to mold Max's natural talents into a well-behaved family dog. Yet his puppy exuberance and occasional stubbornness tested my patience many days! With persistence and an open mind, I learned how to inspire Max's cooperation using positive reinforcement, structure, and clear communication.

Over months of diligent training and socialization, Max blossomed from a rambunctious fur ball into a trusted companion who accompanies us everywhere. His intuition, focus and friendliness never cease to amaze me when we're out in public. The children adore acting as his "co-trainers" for new tricks and commands using reward-based methods.

Today, I cannot imagine life without our charming Labradoodle along for the journey. The lessons and insights I've gained through Max inspired me to write this book - to empower other dog lovers with proven techniques for molding their own brilliant companion. The intelligence and heart that make Labradoodles shine is there within every pup. Now let me share how you can unleash that unlimited potential...

Chapter One

Understanding the Labradoodle

History of the Breed

The Labradoodle is a relatively young breed that was originally produced in Australia around the late 1980s. The goal was to create a knowledgeable, non-shedding guide dog for persons with impairments who suffered from dog allergies. The pioneer of early Labradoodle breeding was Wally Conron, who worked as a breeding manager for the Royal Guide Dogs Association of Australia.

Conron had the idea to cross-breed a Labrador Retriever with a Standard Poodle, which would presumably merge the amiable, trainable nature of the Lab with the hypoallergenic coat features of the Poodle. In 1989, Conron arranged for a Labrador female from the Guiding Dog Association to be bred with a Standard Poodle male that belonged to a local breeder. The outcome was a litter of three puppies that demonstrated ideal features from both parent breeds. The most promising pup was kept for guide dog training and was a big success, indicating the method could work.

Based on this first success, Conron conducted breedings over the next decade to stabilize the hybrid and establish Labradoodles as a breed in their own right. Australian, British, and North American breeders got engaged, utilizing both Labradors and Poodles from guide dog lines to select for health, intelligence, and temperament. Different breeding combinations arose including Labradoodles, F1 crossings, F1bs, multigenerational, and Australian or American lineages.

Popularity for Labradoodles grew in the early 2000s as people learned about their dependable temperaments and coat features. Demand became so great that rogue breeders got involved, damaging the breed's image slightly by breeding more for profit than responsibly for health and temperament. However, committed breeders have worked hard to standardize the Labradoodle into a well-recognized breed that preserves remarkable trainability.

Today's Labradoodles are lively, affectionate dogs available in three size variants - miniature, medium, and standard. They make fantastic guiding, therapy, service, and family dogs. Although occasionally victims of their own popularity, Labradoodles from respectable breeders are consistently smart, gregarious, and allergy-friendly.

Temperament and Personality

The classic Labradoodle temperament is clever, affectionate, lively, and joyful. Since they were developed from two breeds used extensively for service jobs, Labradoodles are people-oriented dogs that form tight ties with their families. They are diligent listeners, quick learners, and highly driven to please their owners.

Labradoodles are active, good-natured, and get along well with children and other pets when properly socialized. They have an appealing silly personality that makes them the life of any gathering. It's not uncommon for Labradoodles to be downright funny, amusing their family with their clownish antics and zeal for life.

This breed has an intrinsically pleasant personality and adapts quickly to a wide variety of lifestyles. They like participating in any family activities or games they are included in. Labradoodles thrive when treated as treasured members of the family and not confined to the backyard or ignored.

Labradoodles do require a moderate amount of daily exercise and mental stimulation. When their demands for activity and interaction are addressed, Labradoodles are obedient house dogs with moderate energy levels inside. They are not nuisance barkers but will alert bark to anything amiss in their environment. Overall, this breed offers the perfect balance of liveliness and trainability.

Some major personality features that prospective Labradoodle owners should expect include:

- Affectionate and attached to family members
- Energetic and playful when it's time for fun

- Even-tempered and gentle with children
- Eager to please and highly trainable
- Adaptable to both active and peaceful lifestyles
- Moderate energy levels when exercising daily
- Intelligent problem-solving skills

Intelligence and Trainability

Labradoodles are typically considered one of the most intelligent and trainable dog breeds. They inherit their smarts and work ethic from both their Poodle and Labrador parent breeds, which are in the top rank of trainable canines. The hybrid vigor of crossing two purebreds has proven efficient at producing guide dogs with great temperaments and trainability.

Owners commonly describe Labradoodles as "easy" dogs to train since they catch up on cues so quickly because of their intelligence and human-focused disposition. They are motivated by praise, and positive reinforcement training is particularly effective with this breed. In fact, Labradoodles often like learning tricks and challenges to train their brain talents.

The intelligence of the Labradoodle implies they do have strong mental and physical exercise needs. Without appropriate mental stimulation, they are prone to boredom and destructive activities like gnawing. Labradoodles flourish when provided with constant training, stimulating toys, and activities. They are happiest when challenged.

Labradoodles excel in obedience competitions, dog sports, and working positions due to their combination of smarts, athleticism, and desire to work cooperatively with people. They are successfully trained as guide dogs, hearing dogs, therapy dogs, diabetic alert dogs, and more. Their friendly attitude and propensity for learning make them perfectly suited for visiting hospitals and schools.

Key indications of Labradoodle intelligence and trainability include:

- Advanced problem-solving abilities
- Quick learning and excellent memory
- Focus and capacity to pay careful attention
- High motivation to satisfy owners
- Success in canine occupations like guide, and therapy work
- Enjoyment of training games and challenges
- Capability to learn multiple vocal and manual commands

Labradoodle owners should be prepared to consistently engage their dog's brains with training activities, interactive play, and food riddles. This breed flourishes when their intelligence is developed via lifelong learning.

Chapter Two

Preparing for Your Labradoodle Puppy

Puppy-Proofing Your Home

Before your Labradoodle puppy arrives, it is necessary to adequately puppy-proof your home. This entails finding and removing any potential hazards or threats to keep your curious pooch safe. Take the time to observe each room from your puppy's point of view. Anything that could be swallowed or knocked over should be kept well out of reach.

Start by eliminating all unsecured wires, cables, or cords. Puppies love to chew, and an electrical cord could cause serious harm or electrocution. Tuck cables beneath furniture or use cord covers to protect them. Block access behind TV consoles and entertainment centers where dangling wires may be accessible.

Next, look for any tiny objects or clutter on low tables that a dog could swallow. Items like paper clips, rubber bands, children's toys, game pieces, and more can represent a severe choking threat. Remember that anything that can fit inside a toilet paper roll is a potential choking risk. Keep counters and end tables clean of pencils, money, letter openers, and other tiny things.

Block access to trash cans and cover them when not in use. Leftover food, chicken bones, corn cobs, and other objects can create intestinal obstructions or splinter and puncture organs if swallowed. Bathroom trash cans may include dental floss, Q tips, razors, and other dangerous materials as well.

Use cabinet locks, anchoring straps, or latches to secure any cupboards or drawers housing anything harmful if opened - including cleaners, chemicals, or pharmaceuticals. Puppy-proof the laundry room, garage, and basement in the same method. These places certainly include many dangerous substances for puppies like antifreeze, insecticides, paint supplies, and more.

Finally, examine the floors and carpets for any debris or loose materials that could be eaten if mouthed or bitten. Pick up any dropped medications, pins, nails, needles, string, rubber bands, etc. Also, check for any hazardous house plants or flowers that may have fallen to the ground.

Taking time to completely puppy-proof each room will start your Labradoodle puppy out on the right paw in their new home! Be sure to repeat the process as your puppy grows into adolescence and receives access to new areas.

Choosing Supplies for Your Puppy

Selecting the correct supplies for your Labradoodle dog doesn't have to be difficult. Focus on covering the basics including bowls, containment, sleeping area, ID, grooming supplies, and toys/chews. Shop for durability, simple washing, and safety.

For food and water, use ceramic or stainless steel bowls that are substantial enough not to topple over easily. Select a crate large enough for your Labradoodle to stand up, lie down, and turn around once fully grown. The crate can start smaller and come with a divider to modify as your puppy develops. Be sure to bring a washable crate pad and chew-resistant cage toys.

Dog beds should be suitable to your Labradoodle's predicted full-grown size. Look for durable, chew-resistant mattresses with removable and washable covers. A basic collar with an ID tag engraved with your contact details is needed right away for identification purposes. Wait to switch to a more restrictive martingale or training collar.

Grooming products including nail clippers, ear cleaners, brushes, and comb sets can keep your Labradoodle looking immaculate. Invest in stain and odor remover for mishaps during the housetraining process. Stock up on a range of interactive puzzle toys to entertain your inquisitive puppy. Purchase natural chews manufactured from safe components to ease teething discomfort.

Be prepared to puppy-proof your yard as well. Fence off threats like bodies of water, gardens, waste areas, or other hazardous plants. Install locks on gates to prevent escape. Consider an outdoor run if you don't have a fenced yard for exercise and play. Set up a shaded, comfy spot for your Labradoodle to relax or play.

Research must-have puppy products but don't go overboard buying every gizmo. Focus on quality over quantity when preparing resources for your Labradoodle's requirements. Reputable pet stores and your breeder can provide particular advice as well.

Finding a Veterinarian

One of the main tasks in preparing for your Labradoodle puppy is building a relationship with a reliable veterinarian. Your vet will be a vital companion in keeping your pooch happy and healthy for life.

Start your search by asking for suggestions from your breeder, other Labradoodle owners, relatives, friends, or local dog groups. Look for an established clinic with experience particularly caring for Labradoodles and up-to-date knowledge on their health needs. Tour any potential clinics to get a sense of the ambiance and meet the vets before committing.

When interviewing vets, ask questions about their health standards for Labradoodle puppies to ensure they fit with your breeder's recommendations. Inquire about the types of immunizations, preventatives, and screenings they recommend and at what ages/intervals. Ask to meet the personnel and determine how friendly and knowledgeable they seem.

Factor in clinic location and hours of operation. Look for a vet within acceptable driving distance that offers flexible opening hours or emergency treatments. Make sure they have an experienced crew of technicians, experts, and doctors to care for your pup should the need arise.

Examine each clinic's amenities to verify they meet your needs. Look for a pleasant lobby, clean exam rooms, boarding choices for when you travel, and space to sustain a developing, enthusiastic Labradoodle puppy. Don't forget to research pricing and payment alternatives among multiple vets as well.

Schedule an introduction appointment once you select a vet to establish your puppy as a patient. Be ready to offer health history and information from your breeder to enable the vet to properly personalize wellness exam suggestions. With a reputable veterinarian partner, you can feel confident your Labradoodle will receive top-notch care throughout every life stage.

Chapter Three

Bringing Home Your Labradoodle Puppy

The First Days and Nights

The first days and nights following bringing home your Labradoodle puppy will be an exhilarating flurry. With careful preparation, you may set your pup up for success during this important shift. Be ready for toilet accidents, crying at night, pinching, and overall mayhem. Have patience and lavish your puppy with affection while establishing vital habits.

Start by defining a safe confinement zone like a crate or small room when you cannot personally oversee the puppy. This prevents mishaps and destructive chewing. Place wee-wee pads nearby for potty requirements. Use baby gates to block staircases and other hazardous areas. Feed fixed meals on a constant schedule and take your puppy outside promptly after eating, drinking, waking up, and playtime.

At night, place the crate in your bedroom to help your puppy feel secure. Expect some sobbing initially when crated at bedtime – don't give in or this behavior will continue. You can try comforting your puppy with calm words or a tiny treat once initially entering the crate. Maintain your sleep ritual while acknowledging, but not unnecessarily soothing a loud puppy.

Be patient with your Labradoodle puppy as they adjust to their new environment. Accidents will happen, but be calm and immediately remove your pup outdoors when caught in the act. Nipping and mouthing is a natural puppy activity — exclaim "Ouch!", provide a toy, and stop play if biting persists. Reward desired actions abundantly with praise, play, and treats.

In the opening days and weeks, start introducing your Labradoodle puppy cautiously to new sights, noises, locations, smells, people, and pets to aid socialization. Keep experiences brief and positive at the beginning. Provide lots of downtime for naps, play, and cuddling as your puppy acclimates to their new existence. Bonding via rituals, training, and care establishes a foundation of trust.

The initial days with your Labradoodle puppy will demand attentiveness and consistency. With time, your puppy's actual personality will emerge and you'll fall into a rhythm together. Shower your new family members with patience, affection, and training to set them up for a lifetime of happiness in their forever home.

Housetraining Fundamentals

A primary priority with your new Labradoodle puppy is adequate housetraining. Puppies under 6 months old have tiny bladders and inadequate control. Consistent routines, attentive supervision, and positive reinforcement are crucial to avoiding indoor mishaps. Know the principles and be ready for a procedure that takes weeks to months.

Establish a regular regimen with set feeding times and periods of confinement when unsupervised. Take your Labradoodle puppy outside immediately upon entering the crate, within 15 minutes after feeding, after waking up, and following play. Praise and provide incentives for peeing/pooping outside. Limit access to portions of the home until thoroughly housetrained.

When indoors, watch for circling, sniffing, or crouching - swiftly interrupt and rush your puppy outdoors to stress this site is not an approved toilet area. Never scold for indoor accidents. Instead, redirect your puppy outside then clean messes completely with enzyme cleanser to remove odors.

Use confinement when you are gone from home or cannot watch the puppy. Short durations in the crate or a dog-proofed room with pee pads available are safer than unrestricted house access. Follow the one hour in the crate for every month of the puppy's age as a maximum recommendation between potty breaks.

Respond immediately and remove your Labradoodle outside if whining or barking from the crate. Reward toilets outside! Avoid letting your dog roam unsupervised even for brief durations until properly housetrained about 6-8 months old. Patience, supervision, and consistency are crucial.

Accidents will happen, especially in the first several months! Stay calm and understanding — scold or penalize only if you actually catch the puppy in the act of peeing/pooping indoors. Stick to a routine, carefully restrict or supervise while loose, and utilize positive reinforcement to signal that outside is the place to go potty.

Socializing Your Puppy

Socialization is crucial for creating a sociable, confident Labradoodle puppy. Expose your puppy to a wide variety of sights, noises, places, pets, and people in a progressive, positive approach. Take advantage of the important socialization phase between 7 weeks and 16 weeks old when puppies are most receptive.

Enroll in a reputable puppy kindergarten class for supervised play with strange dogs and basic obedience skills. Arrange for friends, neighbors, and relatives to meet your puppy once immunizations allow. Invite vaccinated, gentle dogs over for playdates. Expose your dog to city sounds, unfamiliar items, bustling settings, and more for short, planned sessions with lots of rewards.

Avoid overloading your Labradoodle dog during socialization. Watch out for symptoms of fear such as cowering, hissing, or hiding. Pull back and try an experience again more gently if your dog appears uncomfortable. Always couple new exposures with high-reward snacks, toys, and praise to develop a favorable relationship.

Vary the types of people your Labradoodle meets - men, women, children of varied ages and appearances, persons with support devices, uniforms, or deep voices. The same goes for dogs - introduce cautiously to puppies, big and tiny dogs. Seek out unusual sights like automobiles, bikes, and umbrellas, or noises like vacuum cleaners, sirens, thunderstorms, and crowds.

Socialization is most effective when your Labradoodle puppy is relaxed and engaged with you for support and guidance. Keep experiences quick and fun rather than overwhelming. Proper socialization in the first few months fosters lasting confidence, friendliness, and resiliency when presented with new or stressful situations.

Chapter Four

Labradoodle Nutrition and Healthcare

Choosing a Quality Dog Food

Selecting the appropriate dog food is vital for your Labradoodle's health. Look for high-quality components, suitable nutritional amounts for each life stage, and a formulation suited to your unique dog's needs. Consult your breeder and veterinarian for tailored recommendations.

For pups, use a quality brand of puppy formula. Look for chicken, lamb, or fish as the first ingredient, followed by whole grains, vegetables, fruits, and vitamins. Puppies require increased protein, fat, and calorie levels to sustain growth and development. Feed 3-4 meals every day and transfer steadily to adult food at 12 months old.

For mature Labradoodles, consider a high-quality maintenance formula customized to your dog's size and activity level. Look for meat, fish, or poultry as the first item, followed by whole grains, veggies, fruits, fatty acids, and glucosamine for joint health. Many owners prefer grain-free or limited-ingredient meals. Provide fresh water at all times.

Factor in your Labradoodle's age, weight, health conditions, taste preferences, and sensitivity to particular components when picking a formula. Be aware of boutique, exotic ingredients, or too pricey brands that may not exceed nutritional guidelines. Discuss your dog's individual nutritional needs with your veterinarian.

Read all dog food labels carefully. Look for an AAFCO statement assuring complete nutritional adequacy. Avoid nonspecific items like "meat by-products" in favor of specific entire meats. Seek out natural preservatives like Vitamin E versus artificial ones. Tap into your breeder network for eating experiences with Labradoodles.

When shifting foods, do so gently over 5-7 days, gradually increasing the new while lowering the old. Watch for indicators of intolerance including diarrhea, gas, or vomiting. Be prepared to try a few high-quality foods before finding the best match for your Labradoodle's needs and tastes.

Preventing Obesity and Bloat

Labradoodles are at risk for obesity and hazardous gastrointestinal disorders including bloat. Prevent these major health hazards by healthy food, feeding procedures, and lifestyle control. Know the warning signals to spot concerns early.

The most prevalent nutritional problem for Labradoodles is obesity, mainly due to overfeeding, lack of activity, or high-calorie snacks and table scraps. Establish a suggested daily calorie count with your vet and measure food accordingly. Split food into numerous smaller amounts or use puzzle toys to halt eating. Limit treats and avoid table scraps.

Make mealtimes peaceful by restricting access, interaction, and other environmental stressors during eating. Rushed, agitated eating and gulping air can raise bloat risk. Limit high-fat foods and strenuous exercise around mealtimes as well. Space meals at least an hour before and after high-energy play.

Bloat is a fast accumulation of gas in the stomach that can twist or flip the stomach. It requires emergency veterinarian treatment. Early indicators include restlessness, drooling, retching, and an enlarged abdomen. Carefully monitor Labradoodles, especially at crucial risk phases of growing age, stress, or gastrointestinal difficulties.

Prevent bloat by utilizing elevated, narrow feeding dishes to slow eating. Soak dry kibble in water prior to dishing. Avoid gulping-prone habits including eating too rapidly, exercising before/after meals, or tension at mealtimes. Keep water available but don't allow high-volume drinking shortly after meals. Know bloat indicators and respond immediately if noticed.

Proper nutrition, reasonable amounts, perfect body condition, and stress management are crucial to keeping your Labradoodle fit and away from obesity and bloat concerns. Monitor for any troubling symptoms and maintain open communication with your veterinarian.

Grooming and Dental Care

Labradoodles have significant maintenance demands because of their thick, shedding-free fur. Daily brushing prevents matting and keeps their hypoallergenic coat properties maintained. Provide dental care as well to preserve optimum oral health.

Brushing is a must for a non-shedding Labradoodle coat. Use a slicker brush and metal comb to reach beneath the curly top layer down to the undercoat. Pay extra attention to feathering behind ears, legs, tail, and feet where tangles thrive. Brush every day, including extra sessions during seasonal shedding times.

Bath your Labradoodle every 4-8 weeks with a moisturizing canine wash and conditioner. Dry thoroughly with a high-velocity dryer to straighten the coat and prevent mildew odor. Trim nails, clean ears, and eyes, and brush teeth monthly. Seek professional grooming every 6-8 weeks for trimming and styling of the coat.

Check and wipe your Labradoodle's teeth every day. Use toothpaste and brush made specifically for dogs 2-3 times each week. Provide safe, efficient dental chews to minimize plaque and tartar. Schedule annual dental cleanings with your veterinarian to scale plaque below the gum line and address any underlying dental problems.

Catching tiny mats early before they constrict near the skin avoids pain for your Labradoodle. Keep grooming supplies ready and set aside adequate time for regular upkeep to maintain the beauty and comfort of their coat. Proper grooming and dental care enhance your dog's health and quality of life.

Chapter Five

Training Fundamentals

The Basics of Positive Reinforcement

Positive reinforcement training is the most successful and humane strategy for Labradoodles. This strategy promotes desired behaviors and ignores unwanted ones, fostering a cooperative relationship built on trust. Understanding timing, delivery, and the role of indicators is crucial to maximize effectiveness.

The principle is straightforward — activities that are rewarded will increase in frequency. Reward desired activities from your Labradoodle shortly after they occur with something your dog values like praise, treats, toys, or play. Food incentives give immediate reinforcement for teaching new or difficult habits. Vary and phase out treats over time to avoid bribery.

Proper timing is crucial. The reward must happen within 1-2 seconds of the finished behavior to build the connection. Delayed incentives will just reinforce whatever action immediately preceding them instead. Give incentives before your Labradoodle has a chance to disengage or become distracted.

Use reward markers like clickers or vocal prompts like "Yes!" to pinpoint the precise instant the desired reaction happens. These markers aid the timing of the real award which can take a few seconds to deliver. Consistency, quick timing, and high-value incentives increase your Labradoodle's training progress.

Ignore or quickly interrupt undesired actions without scolding or penalizing your Labradoodle. Unrewarded actions will lessen over time. Manage the training environment to prevent the rehearsal of inappropriate actions. Correct behaviors by temporarily frightening or interrupting, then diverting your dog to do something desired instead.

Stick to positive tactics — punishment can destroy trust, motivation, and the human-canine link. Positive reinforcement produces an enthusiastic, confident Labradoodle who appreciates working with you.

Equipment You'll Need for Training

Having the correct tools on hand will make training sessions with your Labradoodle fruitful and efficient. Assemble a toolkit with basic items including leashes, collars, snacks, clickers, and toys adapted to your individual needs.

For puppies, a lightweight nylon or leather collar and a 4-6 foot leash are useful for establishing walking abilities. Switch to a martingale collar or head halter for improved control regulating pulling during adolescence. Always supervise collars and remove them when crated.

Stock a range of goodies that your Labradoodle finds gratifying. Soft peanut butter or cheese cubes are perfect for first training. Carry small, soft commercial goodies on walks for reinforcement. Vary treats to prevent boredom. Work up to randomly interspersing prizes with praise to keep your dog engaged.

Useful instruments include clickers, whistles, and target sticks to designate desired behaviors exactly. Purchase or construct targets with hands-free leash attachments for loose leash walking training. Bring toys like balls, tug ropes, and squeakers to reward and play.

Set up gates, exercise cages, crates, and collapse-able agility equipment to divide training areas at home and on the go. Mats can identify specific locations for indications like sitting or down. Always pack clean-up products for any incidents!

Invest in excellent, well-fitted equipment suitable to your Labradoodle's size and sensitivities. Replace accessories like collars and leashes as your puppy develops. Different tools complement different training goals. A fully packed toolset prepares you to train in just about any place.

Setting Up the Training Area

Designate places for training sessions in your home, yard, garage, or studio to improve your Labradoodle's learning. Remove distractions and provide clear boundaries to preserve your pup's focus. Use gates, pens, crates, and leashes to keep control and prevent straying.

For pups, use small places like a pen within a room or fenced kitchen area to minimize roaming and promote confinement abilities. Start just 5 minutes at a time initially. Use tie-downs, crates, and leashes to prevent pursuing squirrels outdoors. Be prepared to intercept indoor mishaps!

Eliminate access to toys, food, other pets, televisions, doors, and windows that can jeopardize your Labradoodle's attention. Play crate games and treat puzzles in the specified area to develop pleasant associations. Always end on a success to stimulate future training.

Mark limits using exercise enclosures, gates, or leashes. Use tie-downs, platforms, or mats to encourage staying in a specific location. Employ food lures or goals to encourage concentration on you. Keep sessions under 10 minutes for puppies and prepare your Labradoodle to prosper in the surroundings.

Be prepared to exercise in 1-2 minute bursts in distracting public venues like pet stores. Treat frequently to keep attention. Raise criteria gently in low-distraction places first before addressing high-distraction surroundings with older canines. Setting influences success - customize the training space!

Chapter Six

Potty Training Your Labradoodle

How to Crate Train for Potty Skills

Crate training harnesses your Labradoodle's instinct to keep dens clean to encourage excellent toilet habits. By limiting space, you can teach your puppy to "hold it" for steadily longer intervals. Make the box a secure escape, never punishment, and utilize it to prevent accidents.

Choose a crate large enough for your Labradoodle to stand, lie down, and turn around. Include a nice kennel pad and safe chew toys. Acclimate your puppy carefully, leaving the door open with treats inside to develop pleasant connections. Feed meals inside and make the crate a relaxing sanctuary.

Establish a pattern for taking your Labradoodle to potty just before crating periods. Limit crate time to the puppy's age in months plus one hour. Take your pooch immediately outside upon exit for a potty break. Supervise immediately or restrict when out of the container to avoid disasters.

Never use the crate to penalize potty lapses. Respond matter-of-factly to accidents and reinforce triumphs. Thoroughly clean any indoor messes with an enzymatic cleanser to remove odors. Consider utilizing an exercise pen with pads if you'll be absent longer than bladder capacity allows.

Make the container a secure, cozy area. Place it in your bedroom at night and provide fascinating chew toys inside. Expect some first vocal complaints at bedtime from your Labradoodle dog but don't give in or encourage this behavior.

Be patient and consistent. Expand independence progressively when your Labradoodle exhibits reliable control. Limit food and drink consumption before bedtime crating. The crate inhibits reinforcement of indoor elimination and eases housetraining provided you stick to basic rules.

Managing Potty Accidents

Potty training is a process, so indoor accidents are likely with a Labradoodle puppy. How you address these lapses can affect ongoing housetraining success. Stay cheerful, cleanly eradicate odors, supervise closely, and get back on track soon.

When accidents occur, politely interrupt and promptly lead your puppy outdoors to reinforce where elimination belongs. Use a neutral tone rather than yelling, which can scare your Labradoodle and teach them to hide their faults. Limit reactions to interrupt the conduct, not penalize after the fact.

Thoroughly clean any damaged surfaces with an enzymatic pet odor eliminator. Vinegar, ammonia, and soap do not remove all traces of urine or feces odor. The remaining scents can encourage repeat mishaps in the same areas. Eliminate scents thoroughly before your Labradoodle links any interior spot with going potty.

Prevent such breaches by managing freedom and overseeing more tightly. Revisit housetraining essentials including limiting access, timing food and water, and swiftly responding to pee signals. Rule out medical reasons if accidents persist. Consider documenting incidents to detect patterns.

Reflect on any environmental variables like loud noises, new dogs, schedule changes, or inadequate outdoor access that could be impacting your Labradoodle's pee habits. Ensure you are not enabling behavior that leads to additional mishaps.

Stay positive and be patient — some Labradoodles take 6-12 months to thoroughly housetrain. Consistently reinforce outside elimination and restrict opportunities for mistakes via confinement, supervision, and routine. Accidents are normal, but your diligent management can get everything back on track.

Signs Your Puppy Needs to Go Out

Watch for these common cues from your Labradoodle puppy indicating a need to go potty so you can swiftly direct them outside:

- Circling, rotating or pacing
- Sniffing the floor intently
- Sudden absence from play or activities
- Heading to the entrance or a normal potty area
- Whimpering, barking, or agitation in the crate
- Changes in posture like crouching or squatting

- Tail rising or varying tail motions

Your Labradoodle puppy cannot be expected to notify you reliably at first. Instead, proactively establish toilet breaks based on typical activities like eating, drinking, playtime, waking up, and planned crating periods.

As patterns form, you will notice increasingly definite signs right before your Labradoodle needs to be eliminated. Subtle signals can include moving toward the door, Pacing may imply urgency. Heading to a past accident area is a clear sign of need. Barking or whining from captivity requires a prompt response.

Some Labradoodles have distinctive pre-potty routines like chasing their tail or sniffing a particular location. Learn your specific puppy's unique signals over time. If you suspect a need to go, err on the side of caution and bring your pet outside immediately away.

Prevent opportunities for indoor failures by responding swiftly whenever you see any potential potty signals from your Labradoodle. This constant shapes the habit of eliminating the proper outdoor spot instead. Pay attentive attention, especially during the housetraining phase, to set your puppy up for success.

Chapter Seven

Teaching Basic Cues

Name Recognition

Teaching your Labradoodle puppy their name builds the framework for training and establishes crucially important focus and attention abilities. Make name recognition exciting, gratifying, and a high goal during the first few weeks at home.

Start by coupling goodies with expressing your puppy's name in a cheerful, encouraging tone. When your Labradoodle makes eye contact, praise and treat. Use high-value treats reserved specifically for name-response training. Say your puppy's name before meals, playtime, walks, and any fun activities.

Work on name recognition in low-distraction surroundings first, then gradually push your Labradoodle by adding distance and more distracting settings. Move side to side and use target sticks to teach your puppy to swing around and make eye contact while hearing their name. Reward every effective response.

Be patient and keep training sessions brief. Your Labradoodle puppy has a very short attention span initially. Don't anticipate faultless reactions in highly distracting settings straight away - build gradually in modest increments with lots of praise and prizes.

Make a game out of name recognition. Call your puppy's name then cross your arms and wait for eye contact before commencing play or caressing again. Hide behind items and call your Labradoodle's name so they have to find you out for a reward.

Consistent positive reinforcement for responding to their name strengthens this vital ability for your Labradoodle. Say your puppy's name pleasantly and rewardingly - never in wrath. A good name recognition foundation prepares your dog for learning any cue or trick.

Step-by-Step Guide to "Sit," "Stay" and "Come"

Mastering the basic cues of sit, remain, and come offers critical behavior control for your Labradoodle. Build these starting in your home, then progressively add distractions once solid. Here is a step-by-step guide:

Sit:

1. Hold a goodie at your dog's nose level. Slowly elevate your hand over the head so your Labradoodle tips its nose up and hind end down.

2. Once in sit position, mark and reward. Repeat often, then begin saying "sit" soon before your puppy begins the motion. Reward every successful sat.

3. When your Labradoodle associates the verbal cue with the action, say "sit" first before demonstrating the hand gesture. Reward only sits upon your spoken cue.

4. Gradually phase out goodies, interspersing praise and play as rewards. Practice sits in numerous settings and with increasing distractions.

Stay:

1. Have your Labradoodle sit. Say "stay", take one step back, then instantly mark and reward for staying.

2. Gradually increase the distance and length of the stay over numerous sessions before rewarding. Work up to walking around your seated puppy before returning to mark and reward.

3. If your Labradoodle breaks the stay, quickly say "eh eh" and guide them back into a seat to try again. Require them to hold the stay briefly before rewarding so getting up terminates the game.

Come:

1. Say your Labradoodle's name enthusiastically. When they glance at you, back up a few steps urging them to follow for a reward.

2. Increase distance over time, utilizing high-value rewards and running backward energetically to generate incentives to follow you.

3. Begin adding in the verbal cue "come!" right as your puppy begins moving toward you, then rewards upon arrival.

4. Practice comes recalls from various directions, in distracting surroundings, and when engaging with other dogs or people to prove reliability off-leash.

Troubleshooting Common Issues

Labradoodles excel at learning new habits, but occasionally training obstacles arise. Here are some frequent challenges and answers for sit, stay, and come cues:

For sit:

- Won't sit - Lure and reward in easier situations first. Make sure your puppy isn't overexcited or distracted.

- Sits away from you - Reward only sits straight in front of you. Don't reward sits off to the side.

- Sits slowly - Use higher-value prizes to improve motivation. Mark and reward faster sitting.

For stay:

- Gets up rapidly - Returns to shorter stay periods. Reinforce more before releasing. Require sitting before rewarding.

- Breaks stay while distracted - Practice in low-distraction areas first. Use a leash to prevent rewarding breaks.

- Avoids stay cue - Ensure stay is completely trained in low distraction environments initially. Motivate with play prizes.

For come:

- Ignores come cue - Start closer distances and "come" as the dog moves to you at first. Use super rewards.

- Comes part way, then pauses - Back up energetically to urge full recall. Never reprimand halfway recalls.

- Comes but stays out of reach - Reward every step closer. Practice hand targeting into arms reach.

Pinpoint the issue, alter your training technique, motivate your Labradoodle, and set them up to succeed. Ask your breeder or trainer for help adjusting training troubleshooting methods to your scenario if needed.

Chapter Eight

Socialization and Manners

Meeting New People and Animals

Properly socializing your Labradoodle puppy to new people and animals involves patience and pleasant experiences. Take things easy, look for discomfort, and pair introductions with food and praise to establish lifetime confidence and friendliness.

Start socializing throughout early puppyhood once immunizations enable public exposure. Have friends and family members deliver high-value snacks to your pooch while caressing gently. Invite over-vaccinated, gentle adult dogs at first to display basic greeting manners.

Gradually enhance the diversity of human introductions in terms of age, look, sounds, dress, technology, etc. Silently deliver a treat when approaching potentially stressful stimuli like canes, wheelchairs, or screaming kids. Allow modest, supervised engagement if your puppy feels comfortable.

Use distance and barriers initially for introductions to unfamiliar pets. Watch for stiffening, snarling, or scared behaviors. End on a positive note but don't flood your Labradoodle. Public environments like training seminars provide structured interaction chances.

Let new experiences happen at your puppy's pace without overwhelming or flooding them. Be your Labradoodle's advocate and don't accept pushy interactions. Promptly refocus attention on you if your dog seems uncomfortable or overwhelmed during welcomes.

Frequent positive exposures to novelty during the essential socializing window fosters lifelong confidence and sociability. Keep introducing your Labradoodle to new things throughout their lifetime as well to retain sociability.

Bite Inhibition

Labradoodle puppies explore and play using their mouths, thus teaching soft jaws is crucial. Yelp "Ouch!" and interrupts biting to signal it hurts. Redirect to appropriate chew toys and praise gentle mouthing to promote self-control.

When puppy fangs pinch your flesh, swiftly yell "Ouch!" in a high-pitched tone to convey discomfort. Immediately stop playing and turn aside for 15-30 seconds to show biting ends the fun. Then resume playing quietly. The feedback will teach your Labradoodle to inhibit pressure.

Any time teeth hit flesh, repeat the yelp and play the withdrawal process. Be drama-free - simply a little shriek, then silently withdraw attention. Reward your puppy with praise and resume play when they lick or mouth gently without pinching.

Provide lots of appropriate chew options like rope toys and frozen goodies. Say "yes!" and reward chewing the appropriate foods. Manage the surroundings by redirecting and terminating play before biting starts.

Puppies mouth and nip naturally when overexcited. Structure playtime for brief bursts and insert relaxing periods to prevent overarousal. Gentle handling at a young age is also crucial to developing a soft mouth. Bite inhibition training demands patience, especially between 3-6 months of life during teething. Stay consistent and your Labradoodle will learn to play politely.

Manners for Real-Life Situations

Beyond basic training, your Labradoodle requires coaching on suitable manners for real-world circumstances including meeting visitors, walking peacefully on a leash, and acting responsibly around food, toys, and other dogs.

Use positive reinforcement to shape intended behaviors. For door greetings, teach a "sit" or "place" cue. Reward serenity and ignore the doorbell until released. Teach a solid "leave it" and "drop it" for toys and food.

On walks, train a "heel" cue for maintained attention in distracting situations. Reinforce loose leash walking using high-value goodies. Work on avoiding tugging toward people, dogs, or things of interest.

Gradually expose your Labradoodle to passing dogs and people at a distance that permits continued focus on you. Reward disengaging from stimuli and focusing on your cues. Practice waiting politely before racing through entrances or exiting the car.

Settle exercises improve tranquility for greetings or when food is out. Reward desired slow approaches and lack of springing or mouthing. Always reinforce wanted manners and avoid rehearsal of incorrect behavior through management.

Consistent training in real-world events proof desirable habits for the situations you'll experience daily with your Labradoodle. Manners need practice and patience - keep lessons positive and rewarding. Your dog strives to please you!

Chapter Nine

Leash Training

Introducing the Leash and Collar

Properly introducing a leash and collar is the first step in creating outstanding walking abilities with your Labradoodle. Go slowly delivering goodies and praise for cooperation to develop a favorable relationship right from the outset.

Start with simply fastening on the leash and letting your dog pull it about without resistance when indoors. Reward calm behavior and lack of leash biting with rewards and praise. Lifting or moving the leash slightly can stimulate inquisitive chewing to reward.

Next, pick up the leash but continue coaxing your dog along with you using food rewards. Reward forward speed and lack of resistance to light leash pressure. Keep sessions relatively short and engaging.

Gradually begin holding the leash and initiating slight strain, praising your Labradoodle for surrendering to the pressure and following you. Use high-value goodies and positive compliments to make it fun. Always remove the strain soon.

In later sessions, correlate a cue like "let's go!" with you beginning to walk while giving a slight leash direction. Reward your Labradoodle for staying with you. Keep all experiences good to create confidence and willingness to remain near you on a leash.

Remain patient and make all sessions low-stress while introducing your puppy to their collar and leash. These innovative products will rapidly become connected with pleasurable walks and treats with your positive approach.

Loose Leash Walking Techniques

Teaching loose leash walking eliminates dragging and offers pleasurable strolls with your Labradoodle. Use rewards, redirection, and consistency to reinforce your pooch keeping close without tension on the leash.

Always reward and praise the absence of pulling on the leash - even just brief seconds of slack. When pulling happens, stop movement and call your dog back into an attentive sit. Reward for re-focusing on you.

Use high-value goodies to stimulate attention on you instead of surrounding distractions. Vary pace and direction to keep your Labradoodle engaged.

Keep an enthusiastic, optimistic tone saying "This way!" to redirect pulling.

For persistent pullers, use equipment like head halters or no-pull harnesses to remove the reward of tugging while still enabling freedom of movement. Never use choke, prong, or shock collars.

If your Labradoodle pushes ahead, act like a tree by blocking any forward progress until the rope slackens, then promptly praising and rewarding the loose tension. Keep sessions brief and lively.

With patience and consistency over several walks, your Labradoodle will learn remaining near to you keeps the adventure moving and gets rewards. Make it more reinforcing than the environment to master loose leash skills.

Public Leash Manners

Solid leash manners are vital for bringing your Labradoodle out in public locations including neighborhoods, trails, and pet-friendly establishments. Use structure, optimism, and choice rewards to encourage proper etiquette around distractions.

Start by proofing obedience cues like sit, stay, and heel in low-distraction environments initially. High-value snacks and play rewards boost motivation to focus on you when out and about. Keep a cheerful tone and praise engagement.

Gradually introduce your Labradoodle to passing people, dogs, motorcycles, and cars at enough distance to allow ongoing attention on you and response to stimuli. Reward ignoring stimuli and avoiding straining against the leash.

Let greetings with people or dogs occur solely on your terms after a calm sit or concentrate on you. Politely suggest others not pet without permission so you may decide when encounters occur as a training opportunity.

Bring unique toys or chews dedicated only for public outings to occupy your Labradoodle's mouth and curiosity when sitting and watching the world go by. Make choosing to focus on yourself more gratifying than the environment.

Consistency, patience, and structure in public contexts prove excellent leash manners for your Labradoodle with time. Always set your dog up for success by keeping encounters beneath their threshold and reinforcing desired responses.

Chapter Ten

Building Reliable Recall

Recall Fundamentals

Building a dependable recall, or "come" cue, gives vital control and safety for allowing your Labradoodle off-leash independence. Start in low-distraction situations, employ high-value prizes, and reinforce instantly and consistently.

Begin by shouting your puppy's name eagerly and praising any movement toward you with treats and praise. As your Labradoodle begins associating coming to you with incentives, add in a vocal cue like "come!" just as they start moving.

Gradually increase distance and practice coming from different directions. Vary your tone – shout

"Come!" excited sometimes and adopt a more urgent tone at others. Mix in real-life situational exercises like coming when called away from food or toys.

Reward every recall quickly with food incentives, toys, play, and over-the-top praise. Anything less than a quick, passionate reward might damage reliability. Never utilize your recall cue to terminate fun or for something unpleasant.

A lengthy lead line provides safety yet freedom for practice in new surroundings. Throwing sweets and toys away from you incites pursuing them back for quick rewards. Always set your Labradoodle up to succeed and reinforce coming every single time.

Adding Distractions

Once your Labradoodle displays a reliable recall in low distraction conditions, continue adding moderate distractions including beloved toys, novel items, food, and other calm dogs at a distance.

Proof "comes" reliability around toys and treats by first demanding "drop it" when your Labradoodle has an object, praising the release, and then calling "come." Reward large time upon delivery to you.

Have helpers hold your puppy or enlist calm pets while you practice recalling from small distances. Use long lines if needed to prevent rewarding noncompliance. Gradually raise challenges as skills strengthen.

Test "come" with safety gates open or from partially buried holes in the yard. Advance extremely slowly into more risky freedom - dragging a long line prevents dangerous rehearsing of defying until rock firm in distractions.

Always keep your Labradoodle's safety first. Have them drag a lengthy line even after reaching advanced recall so you can immediately intervene if needed until their response is foolproof. Go gently introducing harder challenges over time.

Troubleshooting Recall Challenges

If your Labradoodle shows unreliable when distractions are added, reassess your approach. Refine basics, motivate your dog, and set them up for success by regulating the environment.

- Reward every recall instantly with candies, toys, and over-the-top praise. If you ever withhold rewards, it weakens reliability by indicating coming is not always worth it.

- Improve reinforcement quality and quantity if your Labradoodle ignores your call or recalls slowly. Show them that listening brings the finest benefits every single time.

- If your pup loses focus on the way to you, cheer them on or back away encouragingly. Never admonish a partial recollection, simply reward every step closer.

- Ensure you have a good foundation in low distraction locations utilizing long lines before offering off-leash freedom. Solid fundamentals are key.

- Keep contact with significant triggers like squirrels or other dogs extremely brief and controlled initially. Avoid permitting chase rehearsal until recall is ironclad.

Pinpoint the difficulty and change your approach based on the distinct trouble places. Persistence, positivity, and prevention pay off for mastering a dependable recall with your Labradoodle.

Chapter Eleven

Addressing Unwanted Behaviors

Jumping, Barking and Chewing

Labradoodle puppies explore the environment with their mouth, paws, and voice, so habits like jumping, barking, and chewing are typical but need direction. Use positive training to shift energy into wanted habits.

Jumping up can seem sweet at first but soon becomes hazardous with size and power. Teach a firm "off" or "feet down" cue. Reward four on the floor with praise, pets, and treats. Turn and ignore jumping until it stops.

Barking is communication, but excessive barking needs supervision. First, address any underlying issues like worry, boredom, or health difficulties. For demand barking, wait for silence to reward tranquility. Use indications like "enough" to interrupt barking episodes.

All pups chew, especially while teething. Provide acceptable outlets like frozen chew toys and praise-appropriate chewing. Use flavor deterrents and supervision to curb undesired chewing. Manage the environment and restrict when you can't actively redirect puppy chewing urges.

Unwanted habits need early positive intervention. Use baby gates, tethers, and crates to prevent rehearsal. Reward wanted habits, halt unpleasant activities, and guide your Labradoodle's energy into useful outlets. Patience and consistency resolve natural puppy behaviors.

Separation Anxiety

Labradoodles build deep relationships with their families and may suffer separation anxiety when left alone. Symptoms include whining, damage, house soiling, and excessive barking solely during absences.

Gradually make your Labradoodle accustomed to alone time with very brief sessions as a puppy. Provide food puzzles, stuffed chew toys, and background noise for comfort and distraction. Always greet low-key upon return.

Start with brief out-of-sight activities in the home, then build up to full absences of just a few minutes to several hours according to age and tolerance. Vary departure and return rituals to reduce tense anticipation.

Signs of stress during your absence need a step back in training. If symptoms only arise when alone, separation anxiety is likely. Seek help from your breeder and trainer to gradually condition comfort while left alone.

In rare circumstances, anxiety medication may be temporarily needed alongside progressive training. Ensure your Labradoodle gets lots of exercise and enrichment when home. Extinguish any reward of nervous behaviors. Separation distress takes concerted training but can be overcome.

Counter Surfing and Other Bad Habits

Labradoodles adore eating and can be brilliant at grabbing meals when your back is turned. Curb counter surfing and other problematic activities with management, obedience signs, and rewarding paws on the floor.

Block all access to attractive counters with baby gates, exercised pens, or crate confinement when cooking. Provide a mat or bed cue as an alternative floor placement that gets rewards.

Teach solid "leave it" and "off" cues using high-value food products. Reinforce avoiding enticing meals within sight and keeping in specified locations away from counters.

Clean up promptly after cooking and never leave unattended food within reach. Use treat puzzles to channel your Labradoodle's food motivation into appropriate puzzle-solving outlets.

Manage the surroundings vigilantly to eliminate rewards for stealing food, searching in the rubbish, or other unwanted scavenging activities. Outsmart your savvy dog by picking up cues through monitoring and submissive alternatives. Consistency cures most negative tendencies ingrained by opportunity.

Chapter Twelve

Advanced Training

Retrieving and Other Fun Tricks

Smart and energetic Labradoodles love learning new skills that push their body and wits. Retrieving improves on inherent talents, while stunts like spinning, crawling, and weaving cultivate coordination.

Start retrieval training by teasing and waving toys until your Labradoodle latches on. Say "Take it", let them hold briefly, then say "Give" and swap for a treat reward when they release. Repeat until your pup understands the take and offers cues.

Work up to tossing extremely small distances and prompting the "take it" cue at launch. Upon retrieval, say "give" to trade for a treat when they yield the thing immediately to your hands. Reward just full take and give cycles.

Increase distance progressively, utilizing high-value rewards for rapid recovery and release. Practice from different orientations and with long grips before delivering. Play tug games as a bonus incentive for bringing stuff directly back to you.

Other entertaining techniques to attempt are spin, army crawl, peek-a-boo, bow, and tickle on cue for interactive games. Hand target training teaches touching nose to palm. Weave legs, tunnels, and cavalettas to promote coordination.

Keep advanced trick training rewarding and fun. Practice brief sessions and continually mix in known habits. Mastery of a range of abilities displays the trainability and adaptability of your bright Labradoodle.

Agility Foundations

Labradoodles love learning by starting agility exercises that push their athleticism and bond with you. Mastering jumping, weaving poles, tunnels, platforms, and toys improves confidence and control.

Start by molding a rock-solid "wait" cue on an elevated platform or board. Use targeting and luring to teach stepping forwards, backward, right, and left onto the platform. Reward concentration during positional adjustments.

Introduce a low jump bar on the ground first. Use goodies and targets to motivate jumping forward over the bar, then reward liberally. Gradually raise bar height as skills strengthen. Remember to always keep early leap heights well below the dog's natural capacity.

Weave pole training begins with just two poles put flat on the ground approximately a foot apart. Lure your dog between the gaps using food rewards to create confidence. Slowly raise poles upright and add more over many training sessions to complete a linear weaving pattern between offset poles.

Cavalettis and small tunnels build familiarity in negotiating new obstacles and surfaces. Hand aim your Labradoodle through soft curved tunnels then straight tubes. Reward boldness and confidence when dealing with unique training equipment and props.

Make everything low-pressure, keeping sessions brief, enjoyable, and entertaining. Let your dog set the pace as new challenges are introduced. Agility foundations build your partnership while giving stimulating cerebral and physical enrichment.

Therapy Dog Training

With their friendly disposition, Labradoodles can thrive at therapy work visiting hospitals, schools, and rehabilitation centers. Proper training equips your dog to manage all settings comfortably.

Socialization to sights, noises, and equipment like wheelchairs, crutches, and oxygen tanks helps accustom your Labradoodle to medical situations. Desensitize them to being touched, hugged, and handled by unexpected people.

Obedience skills are crucial to politely engaging with new individuals. Master loose leash walking, "sit", "down" and "stay" cues around distractions. Train a relaxed "leave it" to disregard food or toys left on low surfaces.

Test your Labradoodle's ability to quietly accept petting from strangers. Watch for any signs of timidity or over-exuberance. Therapy dogs must remain focused on their handler and be able to detach from people upon cue.

Exposure to varied surroundings helps generalization. Practice at playgrounds, schools, nursing homes and hospitals. Ensure your Labradoodle remains under threshold around stimuli that may be present during visits like noisy equipment.

Upon mastery of fundamental tasks, enroll your Labradoodle in a certified therapy dog training program. Skills are examined for certification assuring competence to interact safely with vulnerable populations. With their empathy and trainability, Labradoodles are fantastic therapy dogs.

20 homemade food recipe ideas for Labradoodle with ingredients and preparation instructions

1. Chicken and Sweet Potato Stew

Ingredients:

- 2 cups cooked chicken, shredded

- 1 cup sweet potato, diced

- 1/2 cup carrots, chopped

- 1/4 cup peas

- 4 cups low-sodium chicken broth

Instructions:

1. In a large pot, bring chicken stock to a boil.

2. Add sweet potatoes and carrots, and simmer for 10 minutes until slightly cooked.

3. Stir in shredded chicken and peas, and simmer for an additional 5 minutes.

4. Let cool before serving.

2. Beef and Brown Rice Casserole

Ingredients:
- 1 lb lean ground beef
- 1 cup brown rice
- 1/2 cup green beans, chopped
- 1/2 cup carrots, diced
- 2 cups low-sodium beef broth

Instructions:
1. Preheat the oven to 350°F (175°C).

2. Cook ground beef in a skillet until browned, then drain excess grease.

3. In a large bowl, mix cooked beef, brown rice, green beans, carrots, and beef broth.

4. Transfer mixture to a baking dish, cover with foil, and bake for 45 minutes.

5. Allow to cool before serving.

3. Salmon and Quinoa Delight

Ingredients:

- 2 cups cooked salmon, flaked

- 1 cup quinoa, cooked

- 1/2 cup spinach, chopped

- 1/4 cup broccoli, finely chopped

- 2 tablespoons olive oil

Instructions:

1. In a large skillet, heat olive oil over medium heat.

2. Add spinach and broccoli, and simmer until soft.

3. Stir in cooked salmon and quinoa, stir thoroughly.

4. Cook for an additional 5 minutes, then let cool before serving.

4. Turkey and Pumpkin Stew

Ingredients:

- 1 lb minced turkey

- 1 cup pumpkin puree

- 1/2 cup peas

- 1/4 cup carrots, sliced

- 4 cups low-sodium chicken broth

Instructions:

1. In a large pot, sauté ground turkey until browned.

2. Add pumpkin puree, peas, carrots, and chicken broth.

3. Simmer for 15-20 minutes until vegetables are soft.

4. Allow to cool somewhat before serving.

5. Oatmeal and Banana Breakfast Bowl

Ingredients:

- 1 cup oats, cooked - 1 ripe banana, mashed

- 1/4 cup plain Greek yogurt

- 2 tablespoons honey - 1/4 cup blueberries (optional)

Instructions:

1. Cook oats according to package instructions.

2. In a bowl, mix cooked oats with mashed banana, Greek yogurt, and honey.

3. Top with blueberries if preferred.

4. Serve at room temperature.

6. Turkey and Vegetable Stir-Fry

Ingredients:

- 1 pound turkey breast, thinly sliced
- 1 cup broccoli florets
- 1/2 cup bell peppers, sliced
- 1/4 cup carrots, julienned
- 2 teaspoons olive oil

Instructions:

1. Heat olive oil in a large skillet or wok over medium-high heat.

2. Add turkey pieces and heat until browned.

3. Stir in broccoli, bell peppers, and carrots, and simmer until veggies are soft.

4. Allow to cool before serving.

7. Lamb and Barley Stew

Ingredients:

- 1 pound lamb, diced

- 1 cup barley, cooked

- 1/2 cup green peas

- 1/4 cup celery, chopped

- 4 cups low-sodium lamb or vegetable broth

Instructions:

1. In a large pot, sauté diced lamb over medium heat.

2. Add cooked barley, green peas, celery, and broth.

3. Simmer for 30-40 minutes until the lamb is cooked.

4. Let cool somewhat before serving.

8. Tuna and Brown Rice Salad

Ingredients:

- 2 cans tuna in water, drained

- 1 cup brown rice, cooked
- 1/2 cup cucumber, diced
- 1/4 cup carrots, grated
- 2 tablespoons parsley, chopped

Instructions:

1. In a large bowl, combine tuna, cooked brown rice, cucumber, carrots, and parsley.

2. Mix well until components are uniformly distributed.

3. Serve at room temperature.

9. Pork and Apple Casserole

Ingredients:
- 1 lb pork loin, cubed
- 2 apples, peeled and diced
- 1/2 cup green beans, sliced
- 1/4 cup sweet potatoes, diced
- 2 cups low-sodium pork or veggie broth

Instructions:

1. Preheat the oven to 375°F (190°C).

2. In a baking dish, put pork loin, diced apples, green beans, and sweet potatoes.

3. Pour broth over the ingredients, cover with foil, and bake for 45-50 minutes.

4. Allow to cool before serving.

10. Chicken and Rice Congee

Ingredients:

- 1 cup cooked chicken, shredded

- 1/2 cup white rice, cooked

- 4 cups low-sodium chicken broth

- 1/4 cup green onions, chopped

- 1 teaspoon ginger, grated

Instructions:

1. In a pot, bring chicken stock to a boil.

2. Add cooked chicken, rice, green onions, and ginger.

3. Simmer for 20-25 minutes until the rice is tender and the congee thickens.

4. Let cool somewhat before serving.

11. Vegetable and Lentil Stew

Ingredients:
- 1 cup lentils, cooked
- 1/2 cup sweet potato, diced
- 1/2 cup zucchini, diced
- 1/4 cup green beans, chopped
- 4 cups low-sodium vegetable stock

Instructions:
1. In a large pot, add cooked lentils, sweet potato, zucchini, green beans, and vegetable broth.
2. Bring to a simmer over medium heat and cook for 20-25 minutes until vegetables are cooked.
3. Allow to cool before serving.

12. Turkey and Pumpkin Meatballs

Ingredients:
- 1 lb minced turkey

- 1/2 cup pumpkin puree
- 1/4 cup oats, finely crushed
- 1 egg
- 2 tablespoons parsley, chopped

Instructions:

1. Preheat the oven to 375°F (190°C).
2. In a bowl, mix together ground turkey, pumpkin puree, ground oats, egg, and chopped parsley until well blended.
3. Roll the mixture into tiny meatballs and set them on a baking sheet lined with parchment paper.
4. Bake for 20-25 minutes until cooked thoroughly.
5. Let cool before serving.

13. Fish and Potato Cakes

Ingredients:

- 2 cans tuna or salmon in water, drained
- 1 cup mashed potatoes
- 1/4 cup green peas
- 1/4 cup carrots, shredded

- 1 egg

Instructions:

1. In a bowl, combine drained tuna or salmon, mashed potatoes, green peas, sliced carrots, and beaten egg.

2. Mix until completely incorporated.

3. Form the mixture into tiny patties and set them on a prepared baking pan.

4. Bake at 350°F (175°C) for 20-25 minutes until golden brown.

5. Allow to cool before serving.

14. Beef and Pumpkin Stew

Ingredients:
- 1 lb beef stew meat, cubed
- 1 cup pumpkin puree
- 1/2 cup barley, cooked
- 1/4 cup carrots, diced
- 4 cups low-sodium beef broth

Instructions:

1. In a large saucepan, sauté beef stew meat over medium heat.

2. Add pumpkin puree, boiled barley, sliced carrots, and beef broth.

3. Simmer for 30-40 minutes until beef is tender.

4. Let cool somewhat before serving.

15. Chicken and Veggie Muffins

Ingredients:

- 2 cups cooked chicken, shredded
- 1 cup mixed veggies (carrots, peas, green beans), finely chopped
- 1 cup whole wheat flour
- 1/2 cup unsweetened applesauce
- 2 eggs

Instructions:

1. Preheat the oven to 350°F (175°C) and butter a muffin pan.

2. In a large bowl, whisk together shredded chicken, mixed vegetables, whole wheat flour, applesauce, and eggs until well incorporated.

3. Spoon mixture into muffin cups, filling each about 3/4 full.

4. Bake for 20-25 minutes until golden brown and cooked through.

5. Let cool before serving.

16. Veggie and Cheese Omelette

Ingredients:

- 2 eggs

- 1/4 cup mixed vegetables (bell peppers, spinach, mushrooms), coarsely chopped

- 2 tablespoons shredded cheese (cheddar, mozzarella)

- 1 teaspoon olive oil

Instructions:

1. In a bowl, beat eggs until well blended.

2. Heat olive oil in a non-stick skillet over medium heat.

3. Pour beaten eggs into the skillet, swirling to spread evenly.

4. Sprinkle mixed vegetables and grated cheese over one-half of the omelet.

5. Cook until the edges are set and the bottom is golden brown, then fold the omelet in half.

6. Allow to cool somewhat before serving.

17. Pork and Apple Stir-Fry

Ingredients:
- 1 lb pork tenderloin, thinly sliced
- 1 apple, thinly sliced
- 1/2 cup snow peas
- 1/4 cup carrots, julienned
- 2 tablespoons soy sauce (low-sodium)

Instructions:
1. Heat a tablespoon of oil in a large skillet or wok over high heat.

2. Add sliced pork tenderloin and heat until browned.

3. Stir in sliced apple, snow peas, carrots, and soy sauce.

4. Cook for a further 3-4 minutes until vegetables are soft.

5. Let cool before serving.

18. Turkey and Cranberry Meatballs

Ingredients:
- 1 lb minced turkey
- 1/4 cup dried cranberries, chopped
- 1/4 cup oats, coarsely crushed
- 1 egg
- 2 tablespoons parsley, chopped

Instructions:
1. Preheat the oven to 375°F (190°C).
2. In a bowl, mix together ground turkey, chopped dried cranberries, ground oats, beaten egg, and chopped parsley until thoroughly blended.

3. Roll the mixture into tiny meatballs and set them on a baking sheet lined with parchment paper.

4. Bake for 20-25 minutes until cooked thoroughly.

5. Allow to cool before serving.

19. Salmon and Pea Pasta

Ingredients:

- 1 cup cooked salmon, flaked

- 1/2 cup peas

- 1/4 cup carrots, finely diced

- 1 cup cooked pasta (whole wheat or brown rice)

- 2 tablespoons olive oil

Instructions:

1. In a pan, heat olive oil over medium heat.

2. Add peas and chopped carrots, and sauté until soft.

3. Stir in cooked salmon and cooked pasta, and mix thoroughly.

4. Cook for an additional 2-3 minutes until heated through.

5. Let cool somewhat before serving.

20. Chicken and Pumpkin Muffins

Ingredients:

- 2 cups cooked chicken, shredded

- 1 cup pumpkin puree

- 1/2 cup whole wheat flour

- 1/4 cup unsweetened applesauce

- 2 eggs

Instructions:

1. Preheat the oven to 350°F (175°C) and butter a muffin pan.

2. In a large bowl, whisk together shredded chicken, pumpkin puree, whole wheat flour, applesauce, and eggs until well blended.

3. Spoon mixture into muffin cups, filling each about 3/4 full.

4. Bake for 20-25 minutes until golden brown and cooked through.

5. Let cool before serving.

www.ingramcontent.com/pod-product-compliance
Lightning Source LLC
Chambersburg PA
CBHW070814260726
48660CB00005B/1851